Creative Crafts

Paints

Henry Pluckrose

Photography: Chris Fairclough

W
FRANKLIN WATTS
LONDON•SYDNEY

This edition 2004

Franklin Watts
96 Leonard Street
London EC2A 4XD

Franklin Watts Australia
45-51 Huntley Street,
Alexandria, NSW 2015

Copyright © 1987 Franklin Watts

Hardback edition published
under the series title Fresh Start.

Editor: Jenny Wood
Design: Edward Kinsey

ISBN 0 7496 5899 1

Printed in Belgium

The author wishes to record his thanks in the preparation of this book to: Hillary Devonshire for her help in the preparation of material; Christopher Fairclough for the excellence of his step-by-step photographs; Chester Fisher, Franklin Watts, for his advice and guidance; Roz Sullivan for her careful preparation of the typescript; and all the young people whose work he drew upon to illustrate this book.

Contents

Equipment and materials 4

Getting ready 5

Finger painting 9

Colour 'combing' 12

Applying colour ... with wood 14

... with a roller 16

... with scrap material 19

... with fabric 20

... with a straw 22

... with card 24

... in a splatter 26

Marbling 28

Acrylic colour 31

Acrylic texturing 34

Collage with acrylic colours 36

Collage with marbled paper 39

Using wet paper 40

Bubble patterns 42

Magic pictures 44

On your own 46

Further information 47

Index 48

Equipment and materials

This book describes activities which use the following:

Acrylic (PVA) medium
Card
Charcoal
Clear furniture polish
Cold water paste
Drinking straws
Gravel (or fine sand)
Indian ink
Jam jars (old) for water
Knitted glove (old)
Large water bowl or tray
Lino printing roller (or household paint roller)
Liquid detergent
Marbling colours
Mixing trays
Paint – must be water-based – can be bought as:
  (a) powder colour;
  (b) tempera blocks;
  (c) small bricks or tubes of artists' water colour;
  (d) tubes of acrylic colour (PVA);
  (e) finger paints;
  (f) poster colours;
  (g) texture colours;
  (h) tempera paste.
  Make sure you buy at least these five basic colours: red, yellow, blue, black and white.
Paintbrushes (varying sizes and types)
Palette knife
Paper – cartridge, sugar or construction paper
Paper clips
Pencil
Saucer or plate
Scissors
Scrap material – e.g. pieces of bark, braid, buttons, card, cotton, fur, hair, lace, leather, matchsticks, newspaper and paper scraps of all kinds, paper plates, paper tissues, plastic, raffia, ribbon, sacking, sequins, shells, small stones, sponges, twigs, small pieces of wood, wool
Tablespoon
Texture paste (for use with acrylic colours)
Water

This book has been prepared to encourage you to experiment with colour. The activities and ideas outlined in the pages which follow will help you to discover how particular types of paints behave, the many different ways in which colour can be applied and the kinds of surfaces which are suitable for picture-making.

There is no one way to paint a picture. All artists experiment with colour, shape, pattern and texture. Each uses materials in a personal way.

Once you have learned how materials behave, experiment for yourself. To be creative is not just following instructions. The creative person takes an idea and turns it into something which is his or her own.

Some hints

Before you begin, remember that art activities can be messy!

If you are using this book at home, take all the precautions you would take at school. Cover the table with newspaper and the floor around it with an old cotton sheet or a piece of plastic sheeting (e.g. a large dustbin liner).

Cover yourself too. An old shirt or blouse, particularly if it is too big, will give you excellent protection from top to toe.

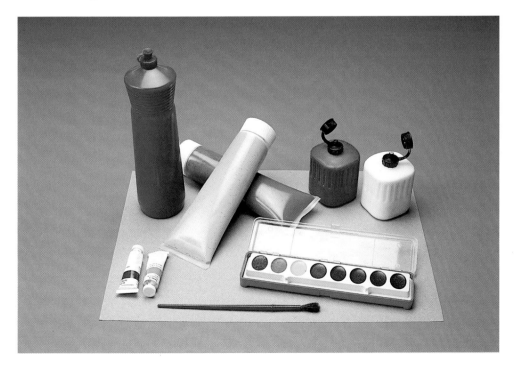

1 Water-based paints are sold in many different packagings. Always read the instructions before you begin.

Your paint

How you use paint will depend upon the type of paint you have. All of the paint colours mentioned in this book are water-based. This means that, to work with them, you will need water.

(a) Powder colour is in powder form and has to be mixed with a wetting agent (e.g. water, liquid detergent) before it can be used. Always add water to powder – never powder to water.

(b) Tempera blocks are solid blocks of colour. The surface of each block needs to be thoroughly dampened before use.

(c) Artists' water colour is sold in small bricks and in tubes. It can be expensive.

(d) Acrylic colour (PVA) is a thick creamy paint, usually sold in large tubes. Acrylic colours have a plastic base and can be thinned with water. Particular care has to be taken when using acrylic paint as its base is also a strong adhesive (glue). When not being used (even for a short period), paintbrushes must be cleaned or kept in water. If this is not done, the brush heads will dry solid. (You can make your own acrylic colours by mixing powder colour with acrylic medium – see pages 31–32.)

2 Colour can be applied in many ways. Notice the range of brush heads.

3 Palettes like these are useful when working with acrylic colour.

4 Bun and cake trays make excellent palettes.

(e) Finger paint colours have been specially prepared for painting with the hands. (You can make your own finger paint mix by mixing wallpaper paste and powder colour – see page 47.)

(f) You can use other kinds of water-based paints (e.g. poster colours, texture colours, tempera paste). Oil-based paints are not suitable for the activities described in this book, except for those on pages 28–30.

Your brushes
Brushes are sold by size. The lower the number (e.g. 2), the smaller the brush. Try to build up a collection of brushes in sizes 2, 4, 6, 8, 10 and 12.

5 Artists' water colour, palette and brushes.

Some brushes are made with a 'flat' tip, some are shaped to a point. Build up a range of brush types.

Brushes are made in different materials. Some (like squirrel hair and sable) are very soft. Others (like hog hair) are hard. Some are made with synthetic materials.

Remember – no one brush is suitable for every activity!

Your paper

Pictures can be painted on almost any kind of paper. The type of paper (or 'support') chosen will depend upon the type of paint being used. For example, thin tissue paper would not be a very suitable 'support' for heavy layers of acrylic paint.

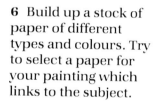

6 Build up a stock of paper of different types and colours. Try to select a paper for your painting which links to the subject.

Finger paintings can be worked with thick pre-mixed paints on almost any type of paper. The most important thing to remember when using finger paint is to work quickly. Marks can be drawn into the paint only while it is wet.

Prints can also be taken from finger paintings.

1 Spread a quantity of finger paint into a clean tray.

2 While the paint is wet, draw a picture into it with the tip of your finger.

3 Place a clean sheet of paper over your picture (the paint must still be wet) and smooth it down with the backs of your hands. Do not press too hard.

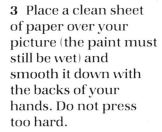

4 Pull the paper away carefully. A print or transfer of the picture will now be on the paper. How does the print differ from the original?

5 This picture, if it is still wet, can also be used to give a transfer. Simply place a piece of paper over it, smooth down and peel off.

6 The finger painting (on white paper) and its transfer picture.

7 *The Scarecrow*
Finger paints can also
be used to make
pictures by painting
with the fingers
directly on to paper.

Colour 'combing'

Finger paint mix can also be used to make attractively patterned paper. When dry, a sheet of colour-combed paper makes an excellent book cover. Before using a sheet of combed paper to cover a book, you will need to 'fix' the colour by rubbing a thin layer of clear furniture polish over the pattern. Make sure the paint is dry first!

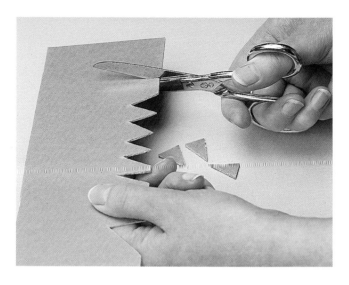

1 Make a comb from card by cutting notches along one edge.

2 Spread finger paint mix into a tray. Draw in it with your comb.

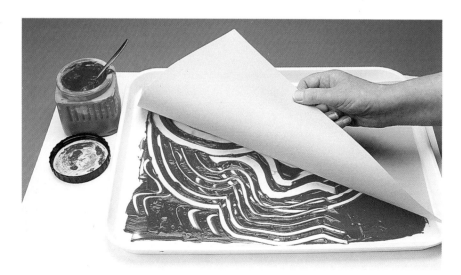

3 While the paint is still wet, place a sheet of paper over the design. Smooth it down lightly with the backs of your hands.

4 The combed sheet.

Applying colour with wood

Experiment to discover how different materials make different kinds of marks in wet paint. Would the soft edge of a feather, for example, give the same sort of line as the piece of wood which has been used to draw the knight shown here?

1 Put two spoonfuls of thick colour on to a sheet of paper.

2 Spread the colour evenly over the paper's surface.

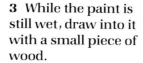

3 While the paint is still wet, draw into it with a small piece of wood.

4 *Knight* Why is it important to choose a paper which is a contrasting colour to the paint?

Another way of applying colour is with a roller. The type shown here is designed for lino printing, but a small household paint roller would do just as well. The roller is used to texture and colour the paper. The texture provides the background for painting.

1 (Above) Squeeze some colour into a tray. Charge the roller with colour and roll it to and fro across the paper.

2 (Below) When the textured paper is dry, paint a design on to it. The design could be made up of simple lines or of blocks of colour.

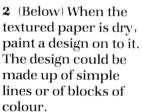

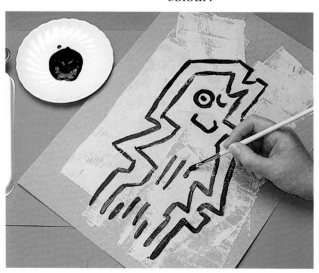

3 *The Old Chair In Sunlight* Here the textured sheet has been used to provide the background for a silhouette.

4 *At the Concert* Here the silhouettes are in two colours.

5 *The Strange Bird* More than one colour can be used for the textured background.

6 *The Park* Here the
roller has been used to
paint most of the
picture – in shades of
green.

Sort your scrap material (see page 4) into several piles. Into one, put all the soft materials (e.g. scraps of wool, fabric, sacking) and into the other all the hard materials (e.g. wood, bark, twigs). Divide each pile into those materials which have a heavy surface texture (like bark) and those which have very little (like smooth plastic). Experiment with the materials you have collected to see what kind of 'mark' they make when used to apply colour. Could you make a picture using only soft materials to apply colour? Could you make a picture using only hard materials?

1 A simple way to charge scrap material with colour is to make a colour pad with a piece of sponge. Place the sponge in a saucer and pour paint on to it. Charge the scraps with colour by pressing them into the paint-soaked sponge.

2 *Wild Cat* This picture was painted using a small scrap of sponge to apply the colour.

Applying colour with fabric

For this activity you will need an old knitted glove. It is easy to apply colour cleanly and evenly with a glove. Try wrapping other kinds of textured material tightly around one hand. Charge your covered hand with colour and use it to produce a pattern. Vary your pattern by working in different colours.

1 Roll out some colour into a tray.

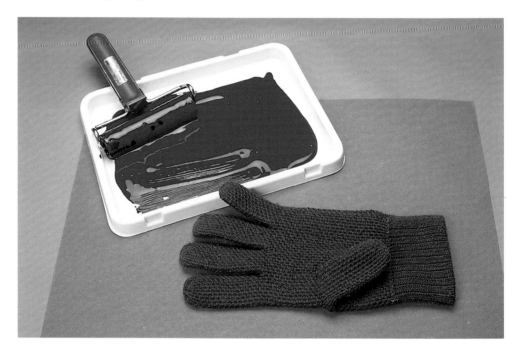

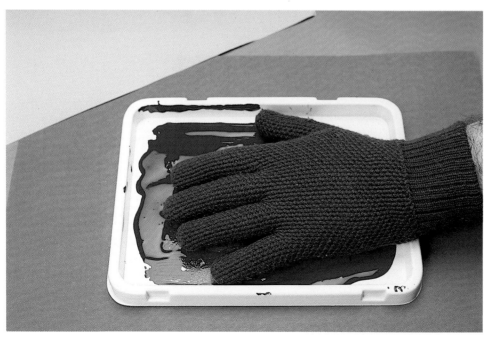

2 Charge the glove with colour.

3 Apply the paint-charged glove to paper.

4 *The Old Glove*
Notice how the paint echoes the texture of the material.

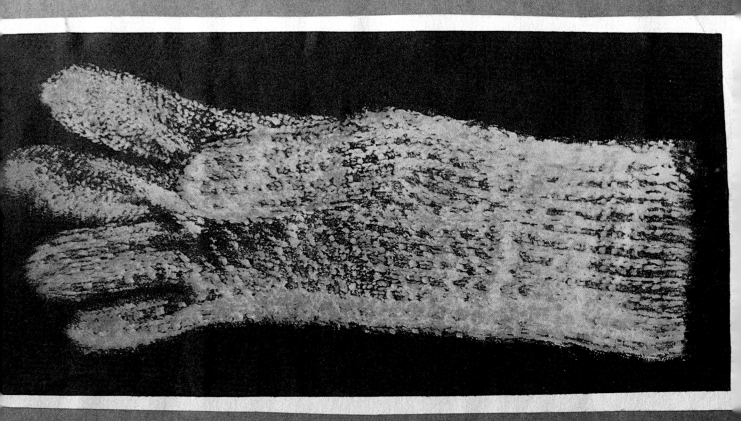

Applying colour with a straw

Pictures can be made by applying colour in tiny dots or spots. A simple way to make a dot picture is to apply the colour with a drinking straw.

1 Place some thick paint into a palette. Here tempera paste has been squeezed on to paper plates – one plate and one straw for each colour. The picture is built up by using the tip of the straw to apply colour.

2 *Church Window* A dot picture painted entirely with drinking straws.

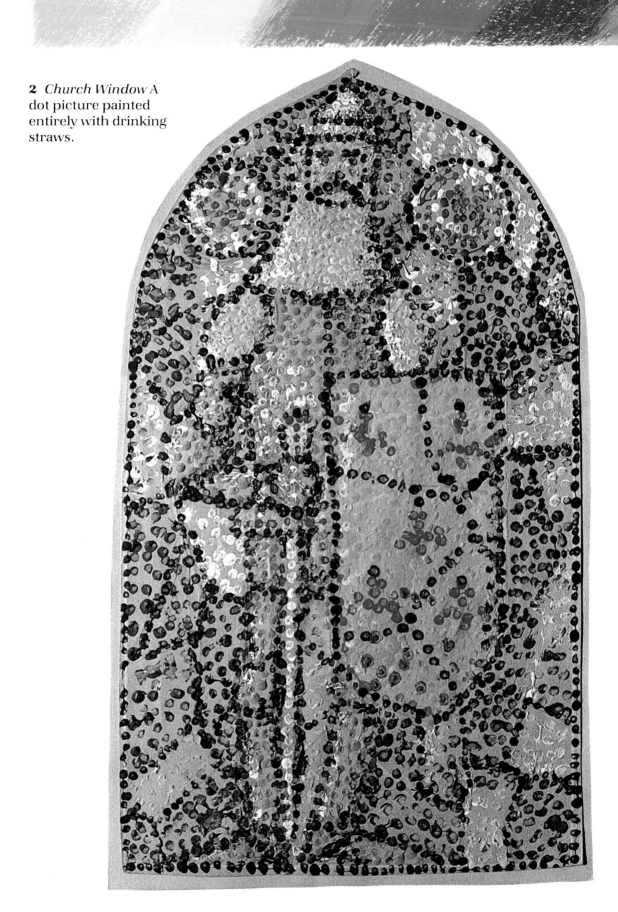

Applying colour with card

As we have seen, colour can be applied with the surface of a piece of cardboard. It can also be applied with its thin edge.

1 Take a piece of cardboard (a postcard will do well) and fold it against itself to make an interesting shape. Use a paper clip to hold the edges together.

2 Charge the edges with colour and use them to make a pattern or picture.

3 *Trees* You could also
try to make a picture
by applying colour
with the edge of an
unfolded piece of card.

Applying colour in a splatter

It's not even necessary always to use brushes, rollers or other materials to apply colour. It can be fun simply to apply colour in drips and in 'worms' straight from the tube. This is sometimes called 'action painting'.

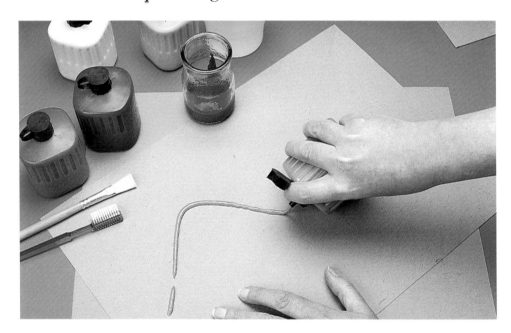

1 Squeezing out the colour.

2 Adding drips of colour.

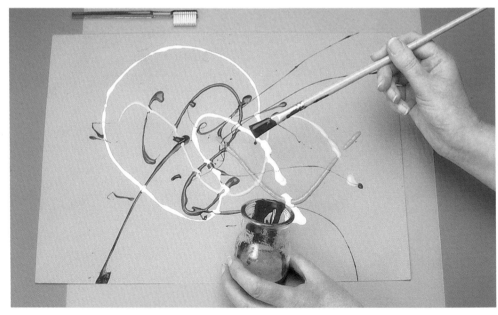

3 *Into Space* A splatter
and drip picture.

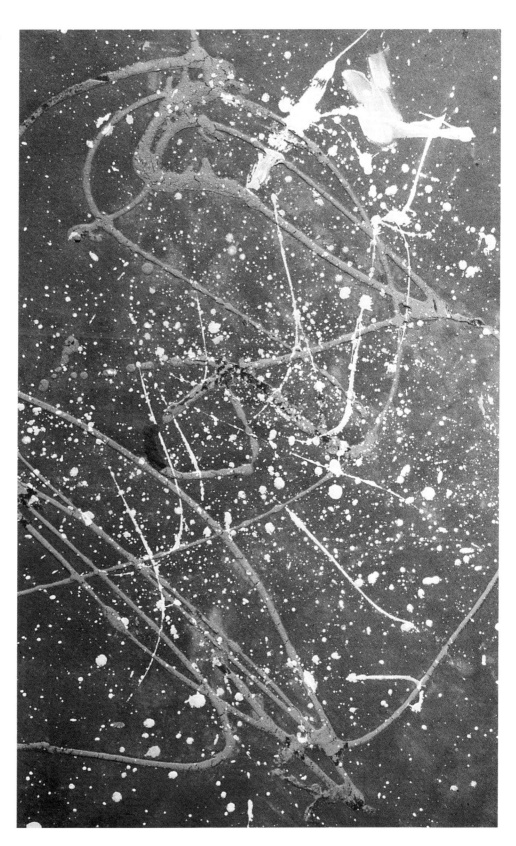

Marbling colours are special oil-based colours. They are used for making patterned papers.

When dry, marbled papers can be used for book covers, shelf and drawer liners, in model-making and even for writing paper.

1 Make sure all the materials are ready and close at hand before you begin. You will need a bowl of cold water, marbling colours, some straws, and sheets of paper on which to work.

2 Using the tip of a straw, drip a few spots of marbling colour on to the water. Use more than one colour.

3 Stir the surface of the water to make sure that the colour spreads.

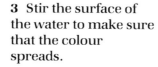

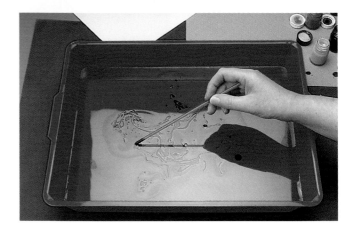

4 Drop a sheet of paper on to the water and leave it to float for a few moments.

5 Remove the paper and leave to dry.

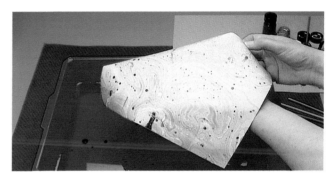

6 A marbled sheet.

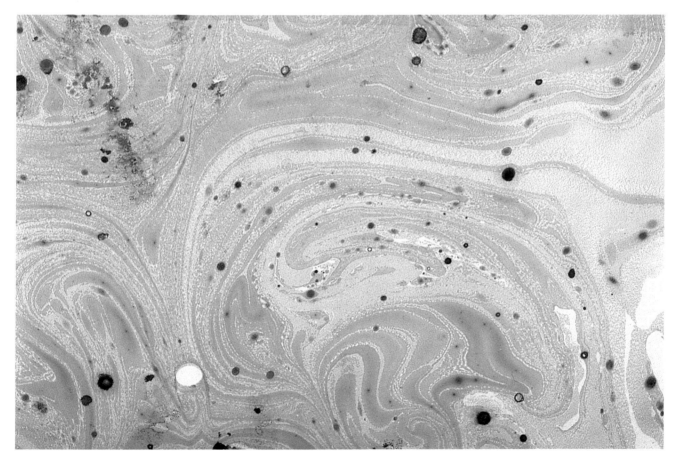

7 *My Friend* Painted on marbled paper.

Acrylic colour

Acrylic colour is a very thick colour and can be applied with brush, roller or palette knife. But the plastic base can be thinned with cold water, so the colour can also be applied in pale colour washes.

Like all water-based colours, acrylic colours can be mixed with each other on a palette to give new colours and tones.

When making a picture with a thick colour, it is wise to work on heavy paper or thin card.

1 Put one heaped tablespoonful of powder colour into a jar.

2 Slowly add water, stirring the powder until it looks like thick cream.

3 Add PVA medium to the paint and water until the mixture is stiff and difficult to stir.

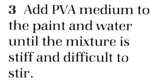

4 Tip a small quantity of colour on to a palette, and paint – perhaps using a palette knife.

5 (Below) *St Paul's* A knife painting in blue and white acrylic colours. Notice how the colour remains textured when dry.

6 *Strange Face*
A painting on card
in acrylic colours and
using a palette knife,
by a girl of three.

Because acrylic colour is also an adhesive, other materials can be added to it to increase its texture. For example, interesting effects can be obtained by stirring fine sand (or even gravel) into the colour before it is applied to the paper.

Some art suppliers sell extenders and texture pastes to use with acrylic colours.

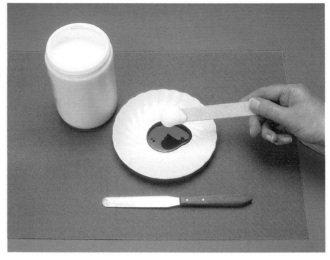

1 (Above) Adding texturing medium to acrylic paint.

2 (Left) Mixing medium and paint together with a palette knife.

3 Painting with a palette knife.

4 (Opposite) *Abstract* A texture painting.

Collage with acrylic colours

A collage is a word used to describe a picture which is made up of scraps of material.

Acrylic colours are also adhesive so if buttons, fabric and paper scraps, matchsticks, sequins, shells, sand or small stones are laid into the paint while it is wet they will stick firmly to it and so become part of the finished picture. The scraps can be given additional texture by overpainting them with acrylic colour.

1 Paint a picture in acrylic colour.

2 While the paint is still wet, add details using scrap material.

4 (Opposite) *The Clown* How many different materials have been used here?

3 Here the collar is being decorated with sequins.

5 *At Sea* Here the picture is made from torn newspaper, a drinking straw and acrylic paint.

6 *A Welsh Lion Called Jones* This picture, painted by a seven-year-old, used cut and torn paper over a thin layer of acrylic colour.

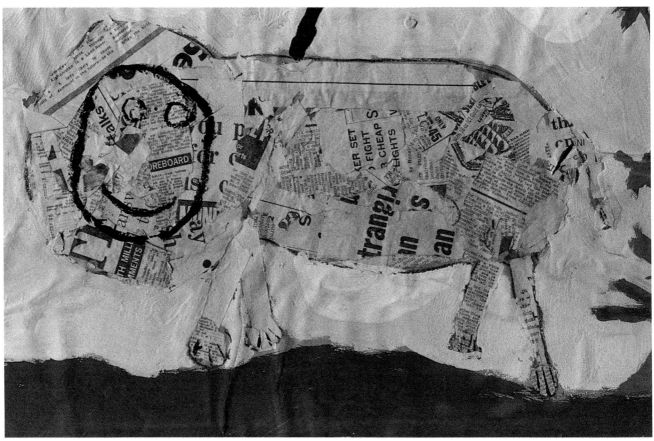

Marbled paper (see pages 28–30) can also be used to make collages. All you need is a selection of marbled paper in different colours. Details can be added in paint.

1 Here a picture of a landscape is being worked. The sheets of marbled paper have been cut into mountain, hill and tree shapes and glued on to a sheet of red paper. Fine details are being added in black paint.

2 *Landscape* A collage in marbled paper.

Using wet paper

Most of the pictures described in this book have been worked on dry paper. Working on wet paper produces quite a different result. You will find that when paints run together new, unexpected blends of colour occur.

1 Thoroughly wet the paper with clean water.

2 Apply washes of colour.

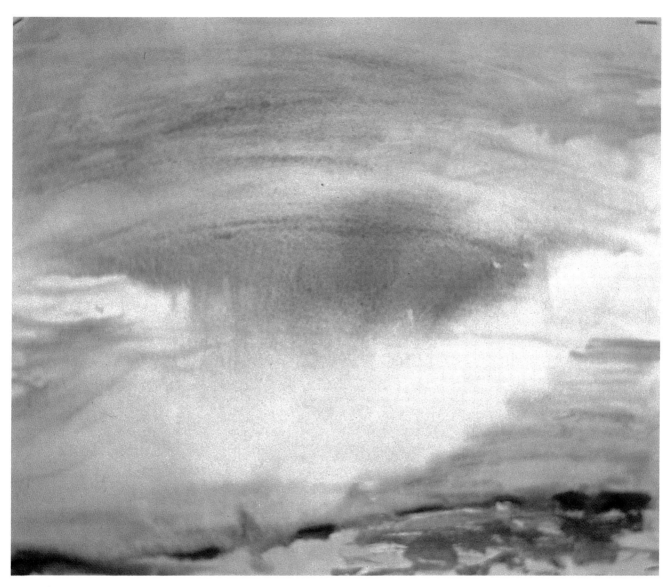

3 *Welsh Hillside* A painting on wet paper by a nine-year-old.

Bubble patterns

This is another way of patterning paper in an unusual way. The papers produced can be used for book covers and for collage.

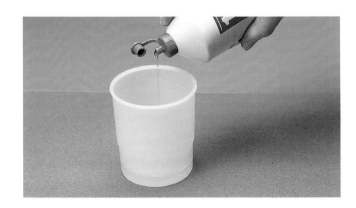

1 Squeeze a small quantity of liquid detergent into a jar.

2 Add a spoonful of wet colour (or Indian ink) and mix them together.

3 Blow into the mixture through a drinking straw until bubbles rise over the edge of the jar.

4 Lay a sheet of paper over the bubbles.

5 The bubble pattern will transfer to the paper.

6 Repeat the process until the whole page is decorated. You could make a pattern in several colours.

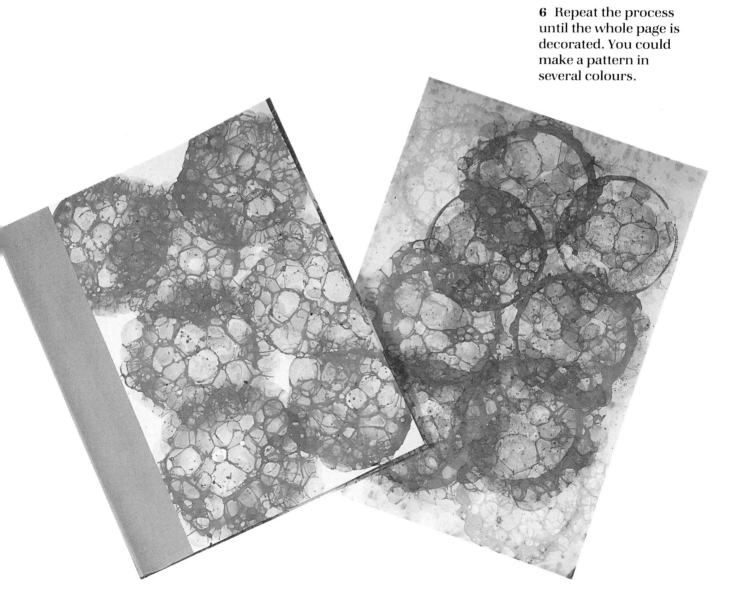

Magic pictures

Indian ink is waterproof. Water-based paint is not. This difference means that these two materials can be used together to produce fascinating pictures.

1 Using water-based paint, draw a picture in lines (i.e. do not fill with colour). Leave to dry.

2 Brush waterproof Indian ink over the painting. Apply the ink thickly but try not to disturb the paint. Leave to dry.

3 Now soak the whole picture in water. With your fingertips, rub the areas you have painted. Because the paint dissolves in water, it will float away, taking with it the covering of Indian ink.

4 When all the paint has been removed, carefully lift the picture from the water. Leave to dry.

Throughout this book you have been experimenting with paints of different kinds. In doing this you will have learned some of the ways in which paints behave. Now try some ideas of your own. Here are some suggestions to help you.

1 Could you make a picture which includes two or more of the ideas contained in this book? For example, could you use marbled paper for a picture worked in acrylic applied with a palette knife?

2 Could you make a picture applying dry powder colour directly on to wet paper? What happens to the colour? How easy is it to control?

3 Experiment by using a technique of your choice on different types of paper. For example, the effect achieved by applying watercolour washes to pastel paper is very different to that achieved by applying watercolour washes to cartridge paper.

4 Try different types of colour for marbling. What is the effect of laying yellow pastel paper in a tray of orange marbling colours?

5 Experiment by using unusual 'supports' (painting surfaces). For example, you could try making pictures on tissue paper, corrugated card, crêpe paper, newsprint, chipboard. How does the painting surface affect your picture, in the way you apply colour and in the paints you use?

6 Use acrylic paint or thick poster colour to decorate and pattern pebbles and smooth stones. Find some oval-shaped pebbles and decorate them with strange faces … or turn them into weird animals and birds. Acrylic colours are excellent for painting on stone. If you use poster colour, protect the design by applying a final coat of thin varnish. Do this when the paint has dried hard!

7 Look in an encyclopaedia for information about Newton's colour wheel. Make a wheel of your own. What does this teach you about colour?

8 Try painting pictures and patterns using a restricted range of colours e.g. blue and white; white and black; red and yellow; blue and yellow; red and blue.

Many stationers carry a range of art materials such as brushes, papers and paints. Some have an art department in which you can buy specialist material like acrylic medium and texture paste.

A useful guide to the stationers and artists' materials suppliers in your area can be found in The Yellow Pages or a Thomson's Local Directory. Look under 'Art and Craft', 'Artists' Materials' and 'Graphic Arts Materials'.

Specialist materials, such as marbling colours, or materials in large quantities can be obtained through a school supplier such as NES Arnold, Findel House, Excelsior Road, Ashby Park, Ashby de la Zouch, Leicestershire LE65 1NG
0845 120 4525
www.nesarnold.co.uk

Acrylic colours and medium

A large range of acrylic colours are available from most artists' materials suppliers.

Acrylic medium (for mixing with powder colour to produce an acrylic paint) can be purchased (at very little cost) in small jars. If the medium is being used for a group activity it is economic to buy it in 1- or 5-litre containers.

When dry most acrylic medium (PVA) forms a waterproof skin, but a range of PVA that will wash from clothes is available.

Acrylic additives

Additives are used to give texture to acrylic colour. They are sold under a brand name. Each additive will be made to a slightly different recipe. Always read the instructions before you begin.

Finger paint

Finger paint can be made by mixing wallpaper paste (available from hardware stores) and powder colour. Add water to two tablespoons of powder colour until a thick cream is formed. In a separate jar, mix two tablespoons of the wall-paper paste with water until a thick smooth cream is formed. Now pour the colour mixture into the wallpaper mixture and stir thoroughly. If the mixture is too thick, add a little water. If it is too thin, stir in dry colour to thicken the mixture.

Acrylic (PVA) medium 4, 6, 31, 47
Acrylic texturing, 34–35
'Action painting' 26
Applying colour 14–27
Artists' materials 47

Book covers 12, 28, 42
Bowl 4, 28
Bubble patterns 42–43

Card 4, 24–25, 31, 33
Chipboard 46
Clear furniture polish, 4, 12
Cold water paste 4, 7, 47
Collage 36–38, 39, 42
Colour 'combing' 12–13
Corrugated card 46

Dot picture 22, 23
Drinking straws 4, 22–23, 28, 38, 42

Fabric 19, 20–21, 36
Fine sand 4, 34
Finger painting 9–11

Gravel 4, 34

Indian ink 4, 42, 44, 45

Jam jar 4, 42, 47

Knife painting 32
Knitted glove 4, 20, 21

Lino printing roller 4, 16–18
Liquid detergent 4, 6, 42

Magic pictures 44–45
Marbling 28–30, 46
Marbling colours 4, 28, 46, 47
Model-making 28

Newspaper 4, 5, 38
Newsprint 46

Newton's colour wheel 46

Paint 5, 6, 14, 15, 19, 21, 22, 36, 39, 40, 44, 45, 46
  acrylic colour 4, 6, 8, 31–33, 34, 36, 38, 46, 47
  artists' water colour 4, 6, 7
  finger paints 4, 7, 9, 11, 12, 47
  oil-based paints 7, 28
  poster colours 4, 7, 46
  powder colour 4, 6, 7, 31, 46, 47
  tempera blocks 4, 6
  tempera paste 4, 7, 22
  texture colours 4, 7
Paintbrushes 4, 6, 7, 8, 26, 31; 47
Paint roller 4, 16–18, 26, 31
Palette 6, 7, 22, 31, 32
Palette knife 4, 31, 32, 33, 34, 46
Paper 4, 8, 9, 11, 14, 15, 16, 28, 29, 31, 34, 36, 38, 42, 43, 46, 47
  cartridge paper 4, 46
  colour-combed paper 12
  construction paper 4
  crepe paper 46
  marbled paper 28, 29, 30, 39, 46
  pastel paper 46
  sugar paper 4
  tissue paper 8, 46
  wet paper 40–41, 46
  writing paper 28
Paper clips 4, 24
Paper plates 4, 22
Pencil 4

Saucer 4, 19
Scissors 4
Scrap material 4, 19, 36
Splatter and drip picture 27
Sponge 4, 19
Stationers 47

Tablespoon 4, 47
Texture painting 35

Texture paste 4, 34, 47
Transfer 10
Trays (for mixing paints) 4, 7, 9, 12, 16, 20, 46

Varnish 46

Water 4, 6, 28, 29, 31, 40, 45, 47
Wood 4, 14–15, 19